THE GOLDEN FLOWER

First-Start® Legends

THE GOLDEN FLOWER
A STORY FROM EGYPT

Retold by Janet Palazzo-Craig
Illustrated by Charles Reasoner

Troll

In a time long ago,
Pharaoh ruled Egypt.
One day, a girl was sent to
the palace. Her name was
Mutemwia. She sang for the
women at the palace.

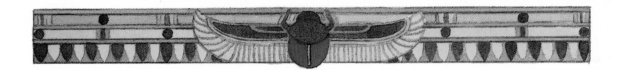

Pharaoh's magician heard the girl sing. He told Pharaoh of her soft music. "Perhaps she can sing my cares away," said Pharaoh.

For many days, Mutemwia sang for Pharaoh. Her music pleased him. Pharaoh also saw that the girl was wise. When he told her of his cares, she always spoke the truth.

One day, Pharaoh was called away.

When he came back, Mutemwia was ill. "Eat and grow strong," Pharaoh told her. "I know you have missed me."

"I have missed you," said the girl. "But even more, I miss my old life. The palace is a cage. I cannot live in a cage, however beautiful it may be."

Pharaoh grew angry. Mutemwia missed her freedom more than she missed him! For many days, he did not see the girl.

The days grew hot and sticky.
Pharaoh was not content.

inally, Pharaoh called for his magician. "I am tired of this hot place," said Pharaoh.

The wise magician knew that Pharaoh missed Mutemwia. He said, "Call for a boat to take you along the cool Nile. Bring a girl to steer the boat and sing for you."

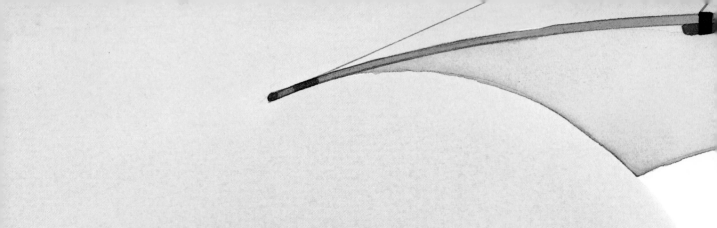

Pharaoh did so. He chose Mutemwia to steer the boat and sing. He ordered a flower made of gold for her hair. He brought the flower to her.

The girl had missed
Pharaoh. When he gave her
the flower, he said, "You are
my truest friend."

The boat set sail.
Mutemwia sang. Cool
breezes blew them along.

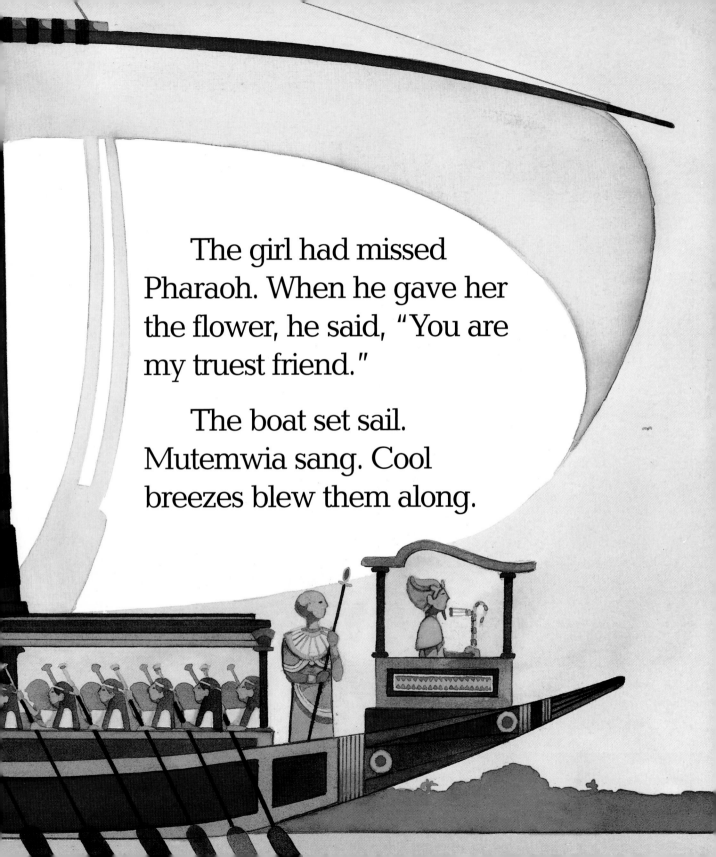

All at once, a strong
breeze lifted Mutemwia's
golden flower from her hair
and carried it into the water.

Mutemwia cried and cried. "Do not cry," said Pharaoh. "I will give you a hundred golden flowers."

"I want only the one you gave me when you told me I am your truest friend," said the girl.

"I will help," said
Pharaoh's magician.

The magician spoke.
Lightning flashed. Suddenly,
the waters of the Nile opened
wide. The boat came to rest
on the dry river bottom.

All were afraid, except for Mutemwia! She saw the golden flower. She climbed from the boat and ran to get it.

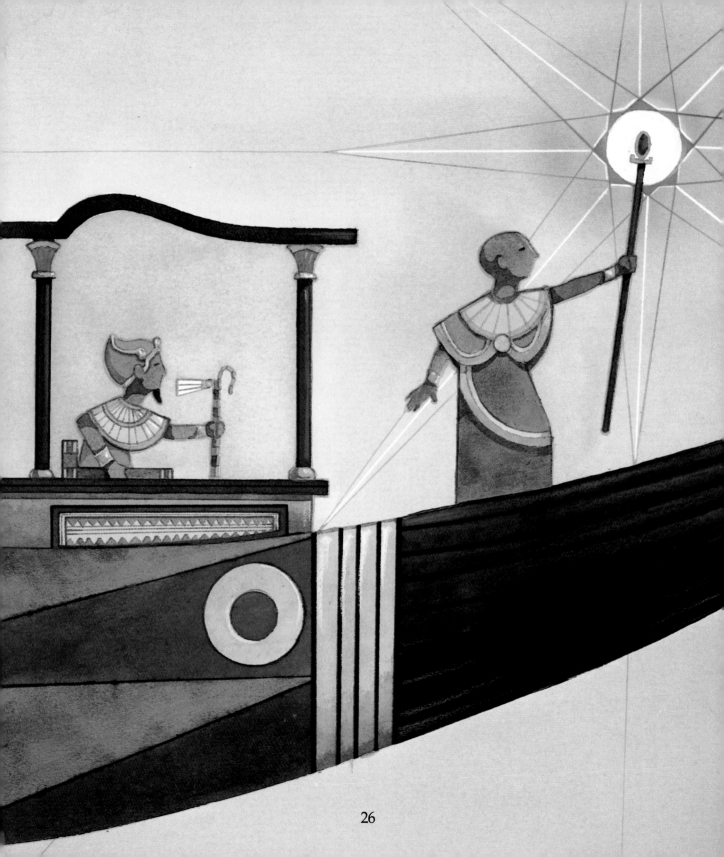

With the flower safely in her grasp, Mutemwia returned to the boat. The magician spoke again. Slowly, the boat rose into the air. The wall of water ran back into the river bottom. The boat sailed on.

Pharaoh looked at Mutemwia. "I now know that I will never lose your friendship," he said. And he gave the girl her freedom.

Pharaoh also gave her a house near the palace. In this way, she could see Pharaoh yet live in freedom.

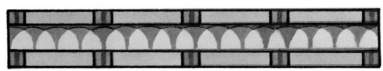

Mutemwia never wore anything in her hair except the golden flower. And Pharaoh and the girl remained honest and true friends until the end of their days.

The Golden Flower is an ancient Egyptian legend. It comes from a story written about 3,500 years ago. The Egyptians of long ago believed that magic could explain many strange things that happened in nature, like the parting of the river in the story.

The Egyptians also believed that the pharaohs were special gods put on earth to rule the people. The pharaoh in the story actually existed. His name was Senefru, and he ruled Egypt about 4,500 years ago. He is famous for building the first of the great pyramids.